340.06 FAU2184

CARSON, GERALD.

A GOOD DAY AT SARATOGA. AMERICAN BAR ASSOCIATION, C1978.

59 P. ILL.

This little book, especially commissioned in recognition of the Centennial Year of the American Bar Association, presents a dramatic and colorful account of the founding of the Association at Saratoga Springs, New York, on August 21, 1878.

The membership of this Association today is justly proud of its long and distinguished record, and its many contributions to the improvement of the justice system.

WM. B. SPANN, JR.
President
American Bar Association
1977-1978

A Good Day at Saratoga

BOOKS BY GERALD CARSON

The Old Country Store

Cornflake Crusade

The Roguish World of Doctor Brinkley

One for a Man, Two for a Horse

The Social History of Bourbon

The Polite Americans

Men, Beasts, and Gods

The Golden Egg: The Personal Income Tax; Where it Came From, How it Grew

A Good Day at Saratoga

"You may, Gentlemen, if you please,
be a vast Accession to the Felicity
of your Countreys . . ."

—COTTON MATHER,
Bonifacius: An Essay . . .
To Do Good (1710)

Collection of George S. Bolster

The Town Hall at Saratoga Springs, New York, where the American Bar Association first saw the light of day. Known today as the City Hall and seat of Saratoga Springs's government, the venerable building, dating from 1871, has lost its clock tower but retains a feeling of gravity and power—and its historic memories.

A GOOD DAY AT SARATOGA

By Gerald Carson

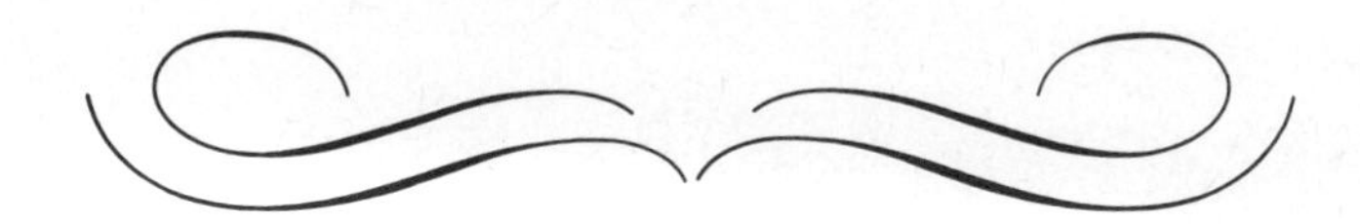

AMERICAN BAR ASSOCIATION

List of Illustrations
xi

A Good Day at Saratoga
1

Bibliographical Notes
55

Town Hall — frontispiece
Town Hall Interior — 5
The Gavel — 9
Simeon E. Baldwin — 18
President Broadhead — 22
Congress Spring Pavillion — 26
Grandstand at Race Course — 30
John Morrissey — 34
Song Cover, *Saratoga Schottisch* — 39
Grand Union Hotel — 47
Grand Union Hotel Dinner Menu — 49

A Good Day at Saratoga

I

On a pleasant August morning in 1878 at the height of the resort season, seventy-five members of the bar from twenty-one states and the District of Columbia gathered in the long, narrow second floor room of the Court of Appeals in the Town Hall (now called the City Hall) at Saratoga Springs, New York. Their purpose was to consider establishing a national association of lawyers. The exact date of this landmark event was Wednesday, August 21, and the auguries were good provided that the expectations were not too great. The groundwork had been carefully laid, the call for the conference drawn up by a skilled attorney. Even nature seemed to smile upon the project. The temperature held in the low seventies. A light northeast wind of four miles per hour rustled the leaves of the magnificent elms which lined Broadway in front of the great hotels with their turrets, mansard roofs and Victorian elegance. Lieutenant

Governor Roger Averill of Danbury, Connecticut, called the meeting to order at ten o'clock.

The summons for the gathering had been circulated to 607 names drawn from forty-one states, territories, and the District of Columbia, so it will be seen that the response was not overwhelming. One recipient of the circular who declined the invitation observed that the meetings would perhaps "be very pleasant," yet doubted "their resulting in any practical benefit." But the response was generally positive. Many letters of encouragement were received from lawyers who for one reason or another could not pledge to attend the Conference but who shared the belief expressed by Professor J. B. Thayer of the Harvard Law School that such an Association could help "in improving the law and legislation of our country."

The seventy-five who did appear and signed the register thoughtfully provided by Simeon E. Baldwin of the Connecticut Bar Association were attorneys of unquestionable professional attainments, men who made waves in their community, state, and the nation. They were deemed to be the organizers of the meeting, for the most part already known to each other personally or by reputation as *vigilantibus non dormientibus*. What they lacked in numbers they made up in quality and that proved to be decisive.

"The suggestion came from one of the State Bar Associations," the circular dated May, 1878, said, "and the undersigned have been favorably impressed by it. A body of delegates, representing the profession in all parts of the country, which should meet annually, for a comparison of views and friendly intercourse, might be not only a pleasant thing for those taking part in it, but of great service in helping to assimilate the laws of the different States, in extending the benefit

Saratoga Springs Historical Society

In this room on the second floor of the Town Hall the conference was held that created the American Bar Association in August, 1878. The scene above is an artist's sketch of a convention of the American Bankers Association, held earlier that same summer.

of true reforms and in publishing the failure of unsuccessful experiments in legislation."

Those who signed the invitation were:

Benjamin H. Bristow, Kentucky.
William M. Evarts, New York.
George Hoadly, Ohio.
Henry Hitchcock, Missouri.
Carleton Hunt, Louisiana.
Richard D. Hubbard, Connecticut.
Alexander R. Lawton, Georgia.
Richard C. McMurtrie, Pennsylvania.
Stanley Mathews, Ohio.
E. J. Phelps, Vermont.
John K. Porter, New York.
Lyman Trumbull, Illinois.
Charles R. Train, Massachusetts.
J. Randolph Tucker, Virginia.

One does not have to be a legal historian to recognize the eminence in the post-Civil War period of many of the names subscribed to the notice. The first two are indicative and Bristow and Evarts happen to have been among the first of those invited to respond to the call. Bristow, a Kentucky Unionist during the Civil War, was the first occupant of the post of United States Solicitor-General and a master of federal jurisprudence. He had been strongly supported by moderate Republicans in the election of 1876 as a presidential candidate and is perhaps best remembered by the public at large for his vigor and success as Secretary of the Treasury in breaking up the squalid Whiskey Ring in the early 1870s. This was a conspiracy of revenue officials and distillers to defraud the government of the internal revenue tax on alcohol.

Evarts, who was currently Secretary of State in the administration of Rutherford B. Hayes, combined two careers as lawyer and statesman. He had also served as president of the Association of the Bar of the City of New York since its founding in 1870 and had participated in many famous cases including the defense of President Andrew Johnson at the impeachment trial. Altogether, ten of the fourteen signatories to the proposal are included in that cross-section of representative individuals who have contributed significantly to our civilization, the *Dictionary of American Biography.*

John H. B. Latrobe of Baltimore, grandson of the engineer who designed the South Wing of the Capitol and rebuilt the "President's House" after the British burned it in 1814, was elected temporary chairman of the Conference. He made a brief address setting forth the favorable consequences which would flow from the formation of the national association. Francis Rawle of Philadelphia, at thirty-two years of age the youngest attorney present, and who gave a lifetime of service to the American Bar Association, was elected temporary secretary. Later Isaac Grant Thompson of Troy, New York, was elected as an additional secretary, both subsequently confirmed as permanent secretaries.

Despite the overwhelming presence of first-class minds well stocked with legal knowledge, or perhaps because of it, some physical symbol of authority was needed to carry on the business of the assembly. For how, after all, can a presiding officer properly discharge his functions without a gavel? But there was no gavel. So the young acting secretary, Rawle, was sent out to a general store, or according to some accounts, a hardware store, where he purchased an ordinary carpenter's mallet for seventeen cents. It performed its first service in the hands of the temporary chairman. Then it passed to Bristow who was chosen permanent president of the Conference. Then it was handed on, like the torch in the ancient Greek games, to James O. Broadhead of St. Louis, who was installed as the first president of the American Bar Association, after the formalities of organization had been completed. His responsibilities as president continued until the next gathering which was designated the second annual meeting.

Widely traveled, heavily used, and not immune to the consequences of hard usage and advancing age, the humble mallet was lovingly bound and capped early in the present century with bands of virgin silver and placer gold from the Pike's Peak region, the gift of the Colorado Bar Association. Inscribed with the names of all the presidents who had held office until its retirement, the old mallet became the revered symbol of an almost apostolic succession. It was used continuously at every annual meeting from 1878 to 1946 and at all midyear meetings from 1936 to 1946. The mallet-gavel is now on exhibition in a glass case at ABA headquarters, a reminder of all the presidents who once wielded it, among them such ringing names as David Dudley Field, James C. Carter, Elihu Root, William Howard Taft, Francis Rawle who purchased it a century ago, and Simeon E. Baldwin, first among equals in founding the Association. The gavel was, for sixty-eight years, as John W. Davis put it in accepting the venerable artifact, "our sole regulator."

Carleton Hunt of Louisiana offered a resolution that a committee of nine be appointed to frame a constitution and bylaws. It is the almost universal practice

This is the famous carpenter's mallet which Francis Rawle purchased for seventeen cents at a store on Broadway at the Springs so that the business of the infant organization could be conducted in an orderly manner. Preserved in this century with bands of gold and silver, the mallet served as a gavel in the hands of ABA presidents at every annual meeting from 1878 to 1946 and at all midyear meetings from 1936 to 1946.

of parliamentary assemblages that he who voices an idea is handed the responsibility for carrying it out. So Hunt was named to head the Committee on Framing a Constitution. But the dominant figure in the Committee's deliberations was Simeon E. Baldwin of New Haven, Connecticut, acknowledged by all his colleagues to be the moving spirit, the Warwick, the inspirer, the committeeman who cheerfully and indefatigably did the camel-driver's work, the veritable founder of the American Bar Association. Of him, more later.

The Committee was instructed to hand in its report at five o'clock that afternoon. It would have proved to be an arduous, perhaps an impossible, task to meet so rigorous a deadline, but for a fortunate circumstance. Baldwin—"Uncle Sim" to his intimates in later years—who well personified the concept of the prudent man, had in his pocket before the Committee began its work, a complete draft of a constitution and bylaws which he had had the foresight to prepare while vacationing in the Adirondacks.

Many years later, Judge Baldwin recalled that he had been simply following the excellent practice of the Reverend Nathaniel Emmons, a leading Connecticut Congregational theologian of the eighteenth century. Emmons said that when an ecclesiastical council was convened he generally wrote out its conclusions before he attended the sessions because, as Baldwin expressed it, the eminent divine found that "this often saved a good deal of trouble and delay." And so it was with Simeon Baldwin's constitution. Only slightly altered, it was ordered to be printed overnight and the freshly-inked copies were ready for distribution at the opening session the next morning at ten o'clock.

There are indications that Baldwin had for some time been turning over in his mind the need for a great national guild of the legal profession. Item, in the fall of 1877, he asked a college classmate, Anthony Higgins, then an attorney practicing in Wilmington, Delaware, for his opinion of the proposal and Higgins encouraged the idea. There is also some reason to think that one or two southern lawyers had approached Baldwin on the subject at a meeting of the Boston-based American Social Science Association which had been held in Saratoga Springs in September, 1877. This Association, which flourished from 1865 to the early years of this century for the study of "the great social problems of the day," included a department for Jurisprudence and took a progressive approach to the amendment of laws. At any rate, among southern lawyers in addition to Hunt who were present at the 1878 beginnings of the ABA were General Alexander R. Lawton and F. P. Poché, all of Louisiana and all of whom were active *ab initio* in the formation of the American Bar Association.

Baldwin faithfully kept a diary for fifty years and may have expanded upon his perception of the need for a national association of the bar in that private place. As to that, we do not know. The diary remained sealed for fifty years. It has now been removed from its tin box and opened but the contents of the diary are not available to historians at the time these pages are written. One can, however, hypothesize some general considerations bearing upon the usefulness of a national bar association, growing out of the spirit of the times. The organizers of the Association were men of the Civil War era. Many had fought on one side or the other. More recently they had survived the country's narrow escape from more violence during the controversey over the contested Hayes-Tilden presidential election. They were eager to get on with the nation's business, to put behind them the memory of Grant's disastrous second administration and the turbulence of Reconstruction. The legal profession was changing rapidly with the railroad lawyer and the businessman-lawyer emerging as the dominant type, keeping step with the emerging interpretation of the due process clause of the Fourteenth Amendment and the needs of the corporate form of organization in the new industrial age. There was on all sides a desire for reconciliation, and on the part of southern lawyers an eagerness to reenter the mainstream of American life. These circumstances help to explain the notably cordial response from the bar of the southern states to the original call.

There was, *inter alia*, an old difficulty, not sectional but national, which a national association might help to remove. As part of the social heritage handed down from colonial times, the lay public retained a latent hostility toward the common law and the profession, a lingering longing for a polity without lawyers, a suspicion that the practice of law was a dark and knavish mystery, a conspiracy to entangle the common man in motions for non-suits, for nolle prosequi, for retraxit, for injunctions, discontinuances and continuances; by oyers, averments and estoppels, using, as one indignant pamphleteer wrote, "hard words, in the Saxon, in the Norman, in the French, in the Latin languages . . ."

This mental "set" among the public at large toward law and lawyers is illustrated in the spirit of antiprofessionalism introduced into the 1851 constitution of the state of Indiana which provided that any citizen and voter could enter into the practice of law upon no other evidence than that of good character. Thus any society or association of lawyers which aimed at raising the current levels of legal training combined in appealing form both idealistic and pragmatic elements. Paradigms already existed in the rapidly-expanding city and state societies, among them being notably the Association of the Bar of New York

City (1870), and the spread of state associations such as Kentucky (1871), New Hampshire (1873), Iowa (1874), Connecticut (1875), and Illinois (1877).

There had been such societies, local law clubs and sodalities as far back as the eighteenth century. Their purpose was to encourage discussion of learned questions and foster a spirit of intimacy, but they disappeared, extinguished by the tumults of the Revolution. Yet the concept of the law as a brotherhood, nourished in England, struck deep roots. Some two hundred American law students had been at the Inns of Court in London before the Revolution, most pursuing their legal studies at the Middle Temple while acquiring also the polish that travel confers upon the traveler and making useful contacts in London law offices. Francis Rawle's grandfather William, for instance, was a member of the Society of the Middle Temple. Sir Edward Coke spoke of the Inns of Court as the English juridical university, for in these ancient houses the students worked together, learned the social graces, performed masques, held revels, and addressed each other as "brother." Lodging and dining together in those dark, four-storied buildings set in a dingy court, young men nevertheless recollected their chambers with affection and pleasure and were powerfully shaped by such traditions as Thackeray invoked when he wrote that a young member passing rooms once occupied by famous men could look up and meditate "Yonder Eldon lived—upon this site Coke mused upon Littleton. Here Chitty toiled; here Barnwell and Alderson joined in their famous labors; here Byles composed his great work on Bills, and Smith compiled his immortal Leading Cases."

James Thackeray, by the way, had studied law before he turned to a literary career.

The original constitution which is still substantially the organic charter of the American Bar Association fixed the name and defined the object as being "to advance the science of jurisprudence, promote the administration of justice and uniformity of legislation throughout the Union, uphold the honor of the profession of the law, and encourage cordial intercourse among the members of the American Bar." The articles provided for a President (not eligible for the office in two successive years), the usual complement of other officers, a Council which managed the nominations for office, an Executive Committee of which Baldwin was a member but not chairman, and standing committees annually appointed by the President for the ensuing year to report on Jurisprudence and Law Reform; Judicial Administration and Remedial Procedure; Legal Education and Admission to the Bar; Commercial Law; International Law; Publications; and Grievances. A Committee on Obituaries was added in 1881 as older members crossed the silent river and ad hoc committees were appointed from time to time to deal with special matters.

There were provisions for local councils in each state headed by a national vice president, which passed upon the election of new members from the state. Candidates could be any person who had been a member in good standing of the state's bar for five years and had also been given the nod of approval by his state Council. In default of such a Council in any state, the candidacy was passed on by the General Council of the Association. Election was by ballot and the dues were a modest five dollars annually.

The American Bar Association was scarcely a monopoly despite the eminence of the individuals who formed it. There were about 64,000 attorneys in the

United States at the time and in many states it was no more difficult to become a lawyer than a doctor. But the Association *was* exclusive. For many years it was easier for a camel to go through the eye of a needle than for a briefless barrister or a brother who practiced advocacy upon a little oatmeal to pass the portals of the Association. Neither gender, race nor religion are mentioned in the Constitution of 1878. But perhaps it is injecting "presentism" into history to expect a declaration upon these matters. In 1878 the questions did not arise.

The bylaws laid upon the President the duty of opening each annual meeting, designated to be held in July or August, with a presidential address "in which he shall communicate the most noteworthy changes in statute law on points of general interest made in the several States and by Congress during the preceding year." The member of the General Council from each state was charged with the responsibility of briefing the President by May in case the legislature of his state had done any significant work. The articles of the Constitution were subjected to a thorough scrutiny, one by one, and stood firm against various proposed amendments, emerging intact except for minute changes. The Committee on Jurisprudence, for example, became the Committee on Jurisprudence and Law Reform. It was decided that the annual meeting would require the presence of twenty members to constitute a quorum and at least the same number voting in the affirmative to amend the Constitution.

It is a measure of the devotion of the members of the Committee on Framing the Constitution to their assigned task that pleasant, sunny afternoon (temperature at noon 78°) that its members stayed with their job, tenaciously deliberating, discussing, proposing amendments and—so well had Baldwin done his work—in the end rejecting them. Thus they missed a high point in the life of Saratoga Springs, the splendid sight beginning at about 1:15 p.m. when the chivalry and beauty of all Saratoga paraded along Broadway under the graceful wineglass elms, past the piazzas of the great hotels and eastward on Union Avenue, the finest drive in Saratoga Springs, in landaus, clarences, phaetons, tallyhos, barouches, simple buckboards and express carts, and in hired hacks ("Cab for the track, sir?").

The objective of the passing show was the famous Saratoga race course where the bugle for the running of the thoroughbreds was blown at precisely 2:15 p.m. As the procession passed, gentlemen raised their hats to fashionable ladies of their acquaintance, to belles in fly-away bonnets driving their own two-wheeled traps or dashing tandems. None were prettier than the nymphs with picture hats and lacy parasols who represented the seraglios of mesdames Grace Sinclair and Hattie Adams. They did not receive or expect the salutes of male acquaintances by virtue of a code that was well understood.

With a card of beautiful horses and a fast track only a mile from the Town Hall, some of those who attended the first meeting of the American Bar Association but were not assigned to committee work must have slipped away to the paddock and grandstand to exercise their judgment of horseflesh. Here is what they saw that afternoon. In the first race (five furlongs) Volturno, a slow starter, passed all the leaders on the home-stretch including Pierre Lorillard's favorite, Boardman, to win by half a head in 1:04 3/4. The second race, a mile and five furlongs, saw Shylock collar the leader at the half-mile and win by a length. Time: 2:57 3/4. Bonnie Wood took the third race easily, a free handicap for three-fourths of a mile. The fourth and last race was a mile and an eighth with five starters for the afternoon's big purse of $800. All the horses were up at the head of the stretch with an exciting finish when Nannie H. won right at the stand in 2:00½.

It was a good day at Saratoga, at the track and at the Town Hall.

Strict chronology will have to yield at some point, and it may best be here, for a quick sketch of the remarkable man who played a dominant role in the early years of the Association, Simeon Eben Baldwin. Physically, he was of slight build and medium height, erect in figure with flowing hair, a longish auburn beard and thick glasses, for he was troubled all through life with weak eyes. Deceptively frail-looking, Baldwin possessed a seemingly inexhaustible store of energy, both physical and intellectual.

Born in 1840 in a substantial, square brownstone house in New Haven, precocious grandson of a judge and son of a Connecticut governor and United States senator, "Sim," as he was called in the family, was already alert to the march of public events by the time he was eight years old. At that time he was deeply concerned that his father, then in the Senate, might vote against the peace treaty designed to end the Mexican War. His mother heard him at his prayers, kneeling beside his trundle bed. And he said: "I thank thee, oh God, that it has not yet been proved that father voted against that treaty."

Following his preparatory school education in New Haven and graduation from Yale, Baldwin studied law at Yale, Harvard and in his father's office. He

Yale University Library

Simeon E. Baldwin of Connecticut, the driving force behind the formation of the American Bar Association, photographed when he was governor of Connecticut with his military aides in the background; hence the brass buttons.

was admitted to the bar in 1863. A quintessential Yankee, Congregationalist, Republican, almost, one is tempted to say, born with an intuitive grasp of the subtle political, legal and business interrelationships of his city and state, Baldwin was recognized by the 1870s as a prodigious worker and master of his profession, carrying a large case-load, and occupying a professorship at Yale Law School. He was, in addition, a historical writer of distinction, an organizer, initiator, civic worker, prolific author of books and articles on important contemporary social issues as well as works of legal scholarship.

In 1884 Baldwin could not swallow James G. Blaine as the Republican nominee for President and led the Connecticut Mugwumps into the Democratic party. Twice Baldwin ran for the United States Senate without success though early in the twentieth century he received consideration as a Democratic presidential candidate before Woodrow Wilson was nominated. Within his own state Baldwin was successful as a jurist, becoming an associate justice, later Chief Justice of the Connecticut Supreme Court of Errors, and when seventy years old he was elected governor of the state. A moving force in countless civic and charitable endeavors, a lifetime supporter of the Yale Law School and active participant in many learned societies apart from his commitment to the teaching and practice of the law, Judge Baldwin inevitably became president of the American Bar Association (in 1890), served as an early editor of the *Journal*, and his name appears on various important ABA committees throughout his lifetime.

Regarded by some as a bit formal and frosty in his professional and public contacts, with a positive take-charge approach to cooperative projects, "Uncle Sim" also had a human side whose memory has fortunately been preserved. He was a genial host and a sought-after guest in social relations, could relish and tell a good story and enjoyed composing a well-turned set of light verses. His loyalty to friends and institutions he believed in became legendary. There are glimpses in various reminiscent writings of this remarkable lawyer-teacher-social scientist-historian pedalling his bicycle along the streets of New Haven in the period when gentlemen wore high hats, his beard streaming out behind. Baldwin's Spartan tastes are reflected in an episode which occurred when as governor he ate his frugal sandwich at his seat in the day coach of a train while his staff regaled themselves in the ambiance of the dining car. Once he walked part of the way to Middletown, Connecticut, to receive an honorary degree from Wesleyan University, partly because he liked hiking and partly perhaps because his instincts for public relations were highly developed.

Simeon Baldwin died in 1927 a few days after his eighty-seventh birthday. He was one of the last three surviving founders of the American Bar Association. As was said at the Commencement exercises at Yale University in 1916 when Baldwin received an honorary LL.D. degree from his alma mater, he was universally acknowledged to be "the first citizen of Connecticut."

III

And now—back to Saratoga Springs. On the morning of the second day of the Conference the newly-constituted Council acted favorably on additional applications for membership and elected officers of the Association for the ensuing year with James O. Broadhead of St. Louis as president and a slate of vice presidents chosen from twenty-eight states and the District of Columbia. Edward O. Hinckley of Baltimore, Maryland, became secretary. Francis Rawle became treasurer. Luke P. Poland, who had been Chief Justice of the Supreme Court of Vermont as well as a representative and U.S. senator, a man of judicial temperament and independent mind, assumed the responsibilities of Chairman of the Executive Committee. A gentleman of the old school, Judge Poland attended the sessions at the Springs in a blue dress coat with brass buttons, velvet collar, and buff vest. Baldwin and William A. Fisher of Maryland were fellow-members of the committee along with the secretary and treasurer as ex officio members.

With the southern wing so strongly represented at Saratoga—there were more members elected from Louisiana than from the state of New York despite the fact that yellow fever was pandemic in the deep South at the time—it was natural to choose a southerner as the first president of the Association. James O. Broadhead was a Virginian who had moved to Missouri and taken a prominent part in keeping that critical border state in the Union during the late War. More recently he had won wide recognition as special counsel for the government in the notorious Whiskey Ring cases in St. Louis which had carried the scandal arising from the distillation of untaxed spirits close to President Grant himself.

The late James Grafton Rogers, Dean of the University of Colorado Law School, in his account of the first fifty years of the American Bar Association, described Broadhead as "a man of the earth earthy . . . a pleasant, big burly sort of man, a sturdy fellow," who was "the great figure of Missouri jurisprudence for nearly two generations;" and Floyd Calvin Shoemaker, historian of Missouri and achievers among Missourians, wrote of Broadhead's handsome

St. Louis Public Library

James Overton Broadhead, congressman, diplomat, a country lawyer who won a national reputation and was chosen to be the first president of the American Bar Association. His face was said to be as good as other men's affidavits.

appearance, genial and open manner and forceful speech. Broadhead has been rated as no great brain but interesting, memorable and colorful as a personality. In origin he was a rather old-fashioned practitioner whose experience harked back to the days when a country lawyer received a dollar for advice, two-fifty for drawing a deed, bond, mortgage and agreement. Ten dollars was considered to be a good fee for trying an action for forcible entry and detainer and a typical private law library consisted of the Revised Code of 1835, Blackstone's *Commentaries*, and Chitty's *Pleadings*. A man of courage, without malice or guile, Jim, or sometimes "Colonel," Broadhead's strongest card was his leonine character. As Rogers has written, "Broadhead's face was worth more than an affidavit."

President Broadhead described the purpose of the new Association as "a noble one," suggested as a guideline for the future that the American Bar Association should "rather aim to codify and harmonize, than to revolutionize or reform the law . . ." It should "watch the progress of events as they occur, and be ready to act on all matters of importance when the need arrives." If faithful to its objects, the Association, he predicted, would realize its high mission "of promoting the science of jurisprudence."

After Broadhead's short speech there were further elections to the membership, a motion to incorporate was discussed but laid aside and the officers and standing committees entered upon their duties. It was all wrapped up in two busy days. The American Bar Association existed. It had a structure and a purpose. Within the year the ABA enrolled 284 members from twenty-seven states and territories. Before adjourning *sine die* the Association resolved to hold its second annual meeting at Saratoga Springs on August 20, 1879. There is no written record to indicate that the founders of the American Bar Association, who were stopping at Congress Hall where they boarded at a special rate of $3 a day, gathered at the end of their successful day to fete the happy conclusion of their labors. If it was indeed the case that no particular celebration took place, the omission was abundantly rectified the next year and in the years that followed.

A question may arise in the minds of those who celebrate the centennial of the ABA as to why Saratoga Springs held the unique place it did in American social life, and why the members of the Association preferred to meet there for the many years that are known as "the Saratoga period" in the Association's history. The topic leads in several directions, all of them pleasant.

IV

In the second half of the nineteenth century thousands of Americans did not feel that they had "seen the elephant" unless they had experienced the delights of Saratoga Springs. This pretty, upstate New York village with cool, dry, pine-scented air descending from the foothills of the Adirondacks and with spouting medicinal springs so charged with carbonic acid gas that they generated enough pressure to blow a steam whistle, was America's challenge to the famous watering-places of the western world, Baden-Baden, Bad Godesberg, Wiesbaden with its *Selterwasser*, the cure at Vichy, and the like. Saratoga, in addition to its medicinal fame, offered relaxation, a fashionable summer life, a horsey atmosphere when the thoroughbreds were running, and a dash of Monte Carlo for those who required faro layouts, rouge-et-noir, no-limit dice games, and ivory balls clicking on spinning roulette wheels to amuse them.

The medicinal springs bore such names as the Congress, High Rock, the Geyser, Columbian, Hamilton, Putnam, Pavillion, Seltzer, Star, Empire and Old Red. The geology of it was that eons ago a cataclysm occurred, a slippage in the strata of rocks overlying the primordial Adirondack gneisses at what is now Saratoga Springs. Through this crack in the earth's surface the naturally mineralized and carbonated waters of Saratoga reached the surface through more than a hundred springs, each different in its chemical analysis and therapeutic virtues. The waters fitted well into the prevailing system of "shotgun" remedies; that is, being alterative, diuretic, and especially cathartic, they might hit something. So the dipper-boys were kept busy filling the tumblers of those with kidney troubles, skin diseases, liver complaint, dyspepsia, biliousness, acidity, nausea, rheumatism (for there were baths, too), disorders of the bladder, Bright's disease, or just that rundown feeling. Each spring had its own identity. The Champion Spouting Spring, for example, discovered in August, 1871, was especially favored by professional men in sedentary occupations, its waters a reputed cure for an affliction not unknown to trial lawyers, called "clergyman's sore throat." Many western gentlemen, however, declared that for steady drinking there was nothing at Saratoga equal to the medicinal beverage associated with Bourbon County, Kentucky. Those who held this opinion found their favorite medication in liberal supply at the hotels and bars of the little health city.

Saratoga Springs's geological accident was especially esteemed for its carthartical powers, its benign loosening effect operating to offset the results of the heavy

Collection of George S. Bolster

Saratoga visitors lining up to take the waters at the Congress Spring. Its sparkling waters put up in bottles became celebrated throughout the world as being therapeutic, invigorating and a sure "cure" for the overworked stomach, tired blood, and the fast pace of "modern" life as it was lived a century ago.

gourmandizing of the period and the costive effect of city life among newly-urbanized Americans. The Congress Spring water, like the Hathorn, was renowned for its efficiency in this regard, being capable of making its presence felt in fifteen minutes. Colonel William R. "Billy" Travers, wealthy clubman, bon vivant and first president of the Saratoga Racing Association, who gave his name to the famous Travers Stakes, was strolling along Broadway with Evander Berry Wall, known as the best-dressed man in New York, when he met a lady of his social class returning from her morning promenade to the Congress Spring.

"Lovely water," she said. "I've just had four glasses."

Lifting his hat with a courtly bow, Colonel Travers, who had a speech impediment, replied: "T-then, M-m-madam, p-p-pray do not let us detain you."

There were many layers and levels of Saratoga life. Marietta Holley, whose droll sketches of the adventures of "Samantha," identified further as "Josiah Allen's Wife," entertained a large audience here and abroad, described a visit to Saratoga Springs which Josiah and Samantha made despite the fact that no relations on either side of the family lived there. They made their way over uneven brick sidewalks to the pump-room where the boy handed around glasses of the pearly water. Josiah, who was somewhat close with money, learning that he could drink all he wanted for five cents, proceeded to put down so many tumblersful that the boy began to look frightened. Samantha recorded the incident with the comment, "he wuz confined to our abode for the rest of the day."

Those who had not been to the Queen of the Spas could learn about the life there and what the waters tasted like from John Godfrey Saxe. Saxe was a

Vermont lawyer and poet who spent twenty-three seasons at Saratoga and was happier in turning out deft verse than in perfecting his briefs. Saxe lightly satirized what he observed at the resort in his *Song of Saratoga.* The visitors, he wrote, ate and ate and ate, flirted, danced the mazy waltz, talked, walked, wooed, wept, laughed, and dressed in the height of fashion. But above all they drank the bubbly waters. Here is what he had to say of them:

Though the flavor is none of the best,
And the odor exceedingly queer;
But the fluid is mingled, you know,
With wholesome medicinal things,
So they drink, and they drink, and they drink,
And that's what they do at the Springs!

Saratoga Springs also gained points because it was easy to reach from the great centers of population. New York was only 182 miles away by steamboat and railroad, with no change of cars during July and August. The resort was 230 miles west of Boston and 274 from Philadelphia. As the train braked its speed to slide along the covered station platform, the towers, mansard roofs, the cupolas and fretwork of the big hotels came into view high above the elms and maples. The brakeman called out "Saratoga," omitting the "Springs" as superfluous, since everybody knew where they were.

The station platform presented an animated scene. Fashionables detraining. Importunate hackmen. Natives staring. Express agents struggling with mountains of the heavy, curved-top, iron-bound Saratoga trunks packed with finery.

Boarding-house porters wearing badges stood under their hotel signs scanning the throng for clients. Informal committees of ladies already in residence met the evening train to estimate the social, commercial, intellectual qualifications, and incomes of the new arrivals.

The visitors divided up according to their destinations. The upper classes registered at the United States Hotel, the Grand Union, or the Congress. The middle class checked in at the Pavillion or Columbian. Those with thin pocket books put up at small, modest boarding houses which could sleep fifteen to twenty guests, offering peace and quiet, low prices, and croquet. Still others found congenial the atmosphere and facilities of Dr. Sylvester S. Strong's temperance and water-cure establishment where the food was blessed and prayers, sermons, and psalms were heard daily; or perhaps they chose Dr. Robert Hamilton's Crescent where the boarders drank the Hathorn water, exchanged symptoms, and a phrenologist felt their heads.

In this mingling of the peoples in an atmosphere of liberty and release, almost of egalitarianism, a thoughtful observer could see in microcosm an exuberant America, sometimes gauche, but frequently gilded. Bookmakers, race track touts, rascals and steerers to gambling houses, with long, dyed moustaches, jostled and rubbed shoulders with statesmen, the aristocracy of the turf, and old society. Health-seekers and tourists joined the classless Broadway parade. Methodist ministers arguing the fine points of Wesleyan theology were elbowed to the curb by high-church Unitarians from Boston and the sidewalk traffic of the beau monde, the demi-monde and rustic visitors in white dusters and paper collars. Dazzled by the afternoon promenade, one enthusiastic writer of the 1870's declared that it was more brilliant than anything to be seen on the Unter

Collection of George S. Bolster

Spectators tense with excitement as the thoroughbreds come down the stretch. This grandstand scene was sketched for Harper's Weekly *by the famous American artist, Winslow Homer.*

den Linden or the Champs Elysées. The chief attraction of Saratoga Springs, as summed up by a friendly English traveler, James Silk Buckingham, was neither the waters nor the salubrious climate. They were "mere excuses for the journey to nine-tenths of the comers." The great charm was "the gay and ever-changing company . . . especially of the opulent classes."

Presidents of the United States from Millard Fillmore to Benjamin Harrison, with the exception of Abraham Lincoln, visited this *sans souci* in America, as well as every governor of New York after 1800. Among men of large affairs who were drawn to the spa were George M. Pullman, William Waldorf Astor, and James R. Keene, speculator and turfman. Leonard W. Jerome, American grandfather of Winston Churchill, was a regular visitor. Railroad presidents yielded to the genius of the place and found it pleasant to gather quietly at the Springs, far from the eyes of the press, to pledge themselves to some new cartel arrangement, usually broken as soon as made. William H. Vanderbilt, apparently unconcerned whether the stock market telegraph indicated a rise or a fall in New York Central and Lake Shore titillated the piazzas as he took his daily drive behind his pair of fast trotters, Lady Mack and Small Hopes, "a pair that can beat the schedule time of many of his railroad trains," the *New-York Daily Tribune* noted.

It was at Saratoga that the American Bankers Association, like the American Bar Association, had its beginnings. Here one could eye John Wanamaker and Edwin Booth, sit at the same table with New Jersey Freylinghausens. Mark Twain came. So did August and Perry Belmont and E. Barry Wall, the dandy and *arbiter elegantiarum*, who was mentioned earlier. Distinguished Civil War military figures visited the Springs as well as the widows of other heroes of the late war. Samuel J. Tilden was there with his pedometer, a regulator of exercise which he never tired of displaying to reporters who would have much preferred to quiz him about the political situation. As a young man, Henry James, the novelist, observed the social scene, called the male guests with their feet on the porch railings, enjoying their cigars and toothpicks, "hard nuts," but thought the dressy women "wonderful."

Philip Hone, once Mayor of New York City, who kept a secret diary recording antebellum life as seen by a socially well-placed citizen, brings Saratoga Springs into focus in saying: "All the world is here: politicians and dandies; cabinet ministers and ministers of the gospel; office-holders and office-seekers; humbuggers and humbugged; fortune-hunters and hunters of woodcock; anxious mothers and lovely daughters;" those in the pink of health and those with "the flickering lamp." As with the legend told of the Cafe de la Paix in Paris, it could be said that if one sat on the veranda of one of the luxury-class hotels at the Springs in the decades of its greatness, sooner or later he would see everybody who was anybody and a good many who were nobody.

And so along with the great and near great appeared the merely notorious. Among the last were James B. "Diamond Jim" Brady with Lillian Russell on his arm; the ineffable James C. "Jubilee Jim" Fisk, looter of the Erie Railroad along with Jay Gould, Fisk in his fustian regalia as a colonel of the Ninth New York National Guard and often accompanied by the regimental band; brevet general Orville E. Babcock, who had been the Whiskey Ring's man in the White House; Coal Oil Johnny Steele, the perfect fool loaded with Pennsylvania oil money; flamboyant and clever Fernando Wood, Tammany Hall mayor of New York; Gould, already mentioned; and a Texan whose name is well lost, flashing three diamond finger rings as he took the waters, also a diamond-and-sapphire scarf pin, and an immense solitaire diamond which he used as a collar button. It was the Age of Diamonds and it had a philosophy: if you've got it, flaunt it.

There was one complex character on the crowded scene who cannot be passed over lightly—tall, dark, and handsome John Morrissey, prize-fighter, gambler, race-track promoter and, to a considerable degree, benefactor of Saratoga Springs. Morrissey graduated from a rough-and-tumble street fighter in Troy, New York, to become an emigrant runner in New York City, then political gang leader and enforcer for the Democracy in city elections, known around Tammany Hall as a useful and promising young man. In 1853 he won a prize fight at Boston Corners, New York, which gave him the title, slightly clouded by a brawl and a questionable decision, to the bare-knuckle heavyweight championship of America. After operating successful sporting houses and saloons in New York City, Morrissey arrived in Saratoga Springs in 1862 with a queenly and dashing wife, an impressive bankroll and social aspirations. He built a casino costing $250,000 and known as The Clubhouse, a luxurious red-brick gambling resort in Congress Park. During his picaresque career Morrissey made and lost several fortunes, was elected to Congress for two terms and sat in the New York State Senate at the time of his death.

In Saratoga Springs Morrissey was genial and discreet. He avoided scandal, acquired the manners and dress of a gentleman, operated his games honestly. He joined in promoting boat racing on Lake Saratoga and together with several wealthy and socially-secure sportsmen was instrumental in founding the Saratoga Racing Association. In addition he put up substantial sums of money for the purses and ran horses of his own. A soft touch for every local good cause—for

Library of Congress

Flamboyant John Morrissey, champion prize fighter, impresario of luxurious gambling establishments, congressman and state senator, was also the founder of the Saratoga Racing Association. His Clubhouse, now known as the Casino, was built in 1870–71, still stands in Congress Park, evocative of the pleasures of the high-rollers of the 1870s.

example, he paid for wetting down the dust of Lake Avenue from the town to Lake Saratoga—Morrissey took money only from visitors, never from native Saratogians. Since the profits of sin were so generously shared with the village, the town fathers allowed the gambling emporium to thrive without invoking the police power against it. But Morrissey's desire for social acceptance was never gratified and on May 1, 1878, at the age of forty-seven, having lived it up, the gambler-statesman-promoter died, just a few months before the lawyers gathered to form their national bar association. Since many of them already knew and appreciated the amenities of life at the Springs, it is not unlikely that some of them shared reminiscences of Old Smoke (a nickname Morrissey acquired from a disreputable episode in his disorderly youth), recalled gratefully the attractions Morrissey brought to enliven the old cure-town, and shared the sentiments of the 15,000 mourners who followed his body to the grave. The newspapers commented extensively upon Morrissey's unusual career and concluded that the world would not look upon his like again. But long before Morrissey gave a fillip to life at the spa, it could lay claim to an eventful and colorful history.

The cascading, saline springs of the Saratoga region attracted wild animals from time immemorial. There Indians, Mohawks and Oneidas, came to hunt them and erect their bark lodges each summer near what was later known as the High Rock Spring. They called the spot Saraghoga, Place of Swift Water.

Or possibly it meant the Place of the Herrings, from the fish that swam up from the Hudson River to Lake Saratoga. On the other hand, the name may have been Se-rach-ta-gue, which would mean, of course, "The Hillside Country of the Great River." No matter; it is all academic now for the Indians cannot tell us and the early settlers were not especially interested or adept in the transliteration of the Iroquois tongue. Let's skip the conjectures and get back to the running story.

In the sixteenth century Jacques Cartier learned from the Indians of the extraordinary medicine spring of the Great Spirit. Father Isaac Jogues, explorer, Jesuit missionary, and martyr, is said to have visited the site as a Mohawk captive about a century later. Another hundred years passed and tradition speaks of a stricken Sir William Johnson, the powerful Superintendent of Indian Affairs for the British crown, being carried by Mohawk braves in a litter to the place of healing waters. Whatever the method of transportation may have been, Sir William certainly was at the site of modern Saratoga Springs because he wrote to General Thomas Gage, then commander-in-chief of British forces in America on September 19, 1771, of "Having lately paid a visit to try the Effects of a Spring lately discovered to the Northward of Schnectady . . ."

Another distinguished visitor appeared at the Springs at the close of the Revolutionary War. In the summer of 1783, General George Washington, having completed and sent off his accounts to Congress and being restless while waiting for the arrival of the definitive peace treaty, made a visit to the New York frontier. Washington was greatly impressed by the springs at Saratoga. Always with an eye for opportunities in real estate, the General, in partnership with Governor George Clinton made an offer to purchase the area. The deal fell through. Washington later expressed to Clinton his keen disappointment "in our expectation of the Mineral Springs at Saratoga."

Soon after, Isaac Putnam, a cousin of the Revolutionary War hero, General Israel Putnam, bought the land around the present Congress Spring, put up a modest hotel, and laid out the village of Saratoga Springs. Hotels proliferated in the early nineteenth century, establishing a faithful clientele and developing the special atmosphere of a resort town. Distinguished visitors appeared early. La Fayette included Saratoga Springs in his triumphal tour in 1825. Joseph Bonaparte, eldest brother of Napoleon I and former king of Naples and Spain, and his sister, Caroline Murat, represented the nobility. Washington Irving; James Fenimore Cooper; Gulian C. Verplanck, lawyer, scholar and author; James K. Paulding, who wrote realistic novels in a sentimental age; and N. P. Willis, poet, editor and social commentator—all brought the cachet which literary figures confer upon a society by their presence, whilst Mrs. Harrison Gray Otis represented the cream of Bostonian whiggism and Madame Stephen Jumel, beauty fading but still a spirited figure spiced with scandal, gave sojourners at the hotels a celebrity fascinating to look at and gossip about.

Saratoga Springs became early on a watering hole for politicians and long served as the informal headquarters for the "Albany Regency," an astute group described by historians as our first political-machine professionals—Martin and John Van Buren, William L. Marcy and their associates, planning strategy and tactics of the Democratic party in the state. Daniel Webster spoke at the Springs in a three-hour oratorical effort in behalf of William Henry Harrison in the hard-fought log-cabin-and-hard-cider canvass of 1840. Three presidential aspirants courted the summer crowds at the Springs that year—Martin Van

Buren, the incumbent President, Major General Winfield Scott, and Henry Clay, the magnetic "Prince Hal," so revered by his admirers that when his name was mentioned, Kentucky Whigs silently lifted their hats. Clay's nimble wit was on display when his opponent, President Van Buren, attempted to pass him in a crowded corridor of the United States Hotel.

"I hope I do not obstruct your way," Van Buren said.

"Not here, certainly," quipped "Harry of the West."

It was also at the same Saratoga Springs hotel that a deliberately-contrived socio-political contretemps occurred. The formidable Mrs. De Witt Clinton, whom Dixon Wecter called "the tyrant of the spa," unforgiving widow of Van Buren's old political rival, publicly refused Little Van's proffered hand and turned her back upon the President of the United States. The occasion, moreover, was a ball given in his honor.

Saratoga Springs held its place in the national affections through the Civil War though there were regrets expressed over the lost patronage of Southern planters and the absence of their ladies, "those very charming Southern ingredients to this most *piquant* of social Salads (Saratoga Springs)," *Leslie's Weekly* —that is, *Frank Leslie's Illustrated Newspaper*—observed. The end of the war brought new people, new riches, a new frenzy for flat racing, and the welcome return of southern visitors. There were new fashions, new money to be spent with a liberal hand, new orchestras discoursing behind the palms, new amusements and sensations, while deft waiters rushed ices and cooling drinks to piazzas or garden courts.

A pattern of life emerged which remained fixed for decades. One sampled the waters before eight o'clock breakfast, drinking to the music of a band, the

New York Public Library

The somewhat idealized scene above appears on the cover of a song introducing a dance, the "Saratoga Schottisch" (sic), and illustrates the hold which the glittering life at the Springs had on the popular imagination in the last century when, according to such graphic representations, men were always handsome, women beautiful, horses spirited, and the waters inexhaustible.

thirsty troops keeping the dipper-boys dipping as each guest chose his spring carefully, two to five tumblersful at the Congress, say, topping off with a glass of iron water at the Columbian at ten o'clock. The ladies walk around the park, bow to the gentlemen, stroll in the parlors, bow again to the gentlemen, have small talk with them and more substantial exchanges with other ladies. Then dress for an overpowering dinner at two. Dress once more for tea. Take tea. Supper at seven. Sit and listen to the band. Dress for the hop, followed by champagne, ice cream and blancmange.

Or one could march around the vast verandas, see and be seen, pick up a novel at the corner bookstore, wait at the depot for the new arrivals, read the *Daily Saratogian*, "a live, spicy journal," it called itself. One could have a likeness taken at Baker & Record's photograph gallery, stroll the entire length of Broadway in about twenty minutes, or if feeling especially fit, walk out to the Glen Mitchell Hotel, a mile and a half north of Congress Spring, then back by the waterworks and Spring Avenue with a stop at Excelsior Park for a last go at the pearly waters.

Indeed, varied opportunities for amusement brightened each day. Those whose taste it suited watched for the funerals, counted the strokes of the sexton's bell which announced the age of the deceased, one stroke for every year of life. Some visitors found it a solemn yet pleasurable experience to repair to Green Ridge Cemetery and contemplate in that marble orchard the shortness of life and its insubstantial vanities, though the sexton also reported a good deal of flirting there and torrid love scenes in secluded portions of the somber place of inhumation. Regattas on Lake Saratoga brought the crews and crowds of university men. Barnum's circus played at the Springs when touring New York

State, and sometimes the town took on a military air when the Worcester Continentals arrived by way of the Hoosac Tunnel for their summer training.

Easy expeditions included a trip to the picturesque Indian Encampment, its white tents gleaming among the hemlocks, where woven baskets, beadwork, and other curios could be purchased. Mount McGregor was another objective and patriots were drawn to the nearby Saratoga battlefield. Gourmets took the omnibuses out to Cary Moon's Lake House at Lake Saratoga where gentlemen with long purses dined on canvasbacks accompanied by Johannisberger. Or one could catch his own trout while sitting in an easy chair, served up later with the famous paper-thin fried potatoes known as Saratoga chips which were created at that very spot by Moon's gifted chef.

So that's what they did, as the poet chanted, at Saratoga Springs, where everyone came for his own reasons—seeking a sea-change among the pines, or for the waters, to throw a card or follow the horses, to marry off a daughter, to take a toddy at sunset, to see old friends, to discuss the state of the nation with respected peers, or just to capture a scene that might quite possibly turn out to be richer in memory than in reality.

For many older lawyers Saratoga Springs brought back sentimental recollections. Until the reformation of the state's judicial system under the constitution of 1846 which merged the practice of law and equity, the state Court of Chancery over which famed Chancellor James Kent had presided was located at the Springs. Then, as later, the mid-summer charms of Saratoga were not lost on judges, witnesses, clerks and counsellors. Henry Wilbur Palmer, a leading trial lawyer of Pennsylvania and the state's attorney general, summed up well the feelings of lawyers still active in the 70s, when he said: "There is something to come here for besides the American Bar Association, and the meeting of the Association affords a very convenient excuse to come to Saratoga."

Early in the 1879 social season the resort-watchers of Saratoga Springs confidently put aside those dark thoughts which sometimes assailed them when word was received of heavy bookings at Long Branch, new attractions installed at Coney Island, or new heights of *ton* achieved at Newport. At Newport, they said at the Springs, one got New Yorkers and a stuffy formality. At Cape May—Philadelphians. In Maine—Bostonians. But at Saratoga Springs the cream of the cream of all joined together to create a delightful cosmopolitan flavor. James Silk Buckingham would have agreed for a generation earlier he had made the handsome declaration that there were present at the American watering-place "quite as many elegant men and a great many more beautiful women than could be seen in the public rooms at Brighton or Bath."

There were substantial reasons for the feeling that Saratoga Springs would continue to compete successfully with any *dolce far niente* which other summer resorts could think up. The United States Hotel had a new skating rink. The Grand Union had greatly enlarged the garden in its interior court which was now brilliantly illuminated with the new electric lamps that glowed even in the rain. Wall Street men were enjoying "flush" times and kept the telegraph instruments chattering in the good cause of increasing their capital. The Republicans had selected the Springs for the site of the New York State Convention and already Chauncey M. Depew, Thurlow Reed, that master of behind-the-scenes maneuvering, Lieutenant Governor William Dorsheimer, and various other stalwarts were refreshing themselves at the spa before the wire-pulling and pipe-laying began. And it was gratefully recalled when John T. Hoffman, former Democratic Governor of New York appeared, that the Tammany sachems from the Fourteenth-Street wigwam always showed up in August, which might with reason be called the Month of the Politicians.

A brass band paraded the streets of the Springs on August 20th advertising the last day of the race meeting. On that day the Association of Stenographers terminated its annual meeting just as the Town Hall received the American Bar Association. Already prominent lawyers were registered at the big hotels. Clarkson N. Potter and Benjamin H. Bristow of New York, General A. R. Lawton of Savannah and Charles A. Broadhead of St. Louis were at the United States. Carleton Hunt of New Orleans was at the Grand Union. The Honorable Judge Poland, Chairman of the Executive Committee of the Association, was on hand and called the meeting to order shortly after ten o'clock with a hundred members in attendance.

The list of members at this time contained 289 names. Two hundred and one were elected at this meeting, bringing the total to 490, less a few deaths and resignations. The Executive Committee reported that it had made a number of changes in the bylaws. One would permit each state bar association to be represented through delegates at all meetings of the national association. Another bylaw was adopted permitting members of the bar of any foreign country, or of any state, who were not members of the ABA, to be admitted to the privileges of the floor.

The Report of the Committee on Legal Education and Admission to the Bar is an example of the serious work undertaken in the formative years of the ABA. It traced the progress of legal education historically from the time of Justinian, through the Middle Ages, the Renaissance in western Europe and down to the contemporary situation, set forth with much erudition and the literary decoration in vogue at the time: "The broken columns still mark the place where the Roman forum once stood," and where "the accents of Cicero breathed and burned." The Report concluded by presenting courses of study which were recommended to state and local bar associations as minimum educational standards for admission to the practice of law; and a resolution was presented and passed recommending that the states maintain by public authority schools of law "provided with faculties of at least four well paid and efficient teachers . . ."

It was decided to employ a stenographer at each annual meeting and that no person would be allowed to speak more than ten minutes at a time or more than twice on one subject. Finally, the Association adopted a resolution presented by the Committee on Jurisprudence and Law Reform calling for state action to secure through legislation uniformity in legal instruments affecting real estate and the mode of executing and attesting wills. The same Committee was asked to present at the next annual meeting a synopsis of the marriage and divorce laws of the various states with a view of procuring uniform legislation affecting these matters.

Substantial papers dealing with important technical topics were read: Henry Hitchcock (Missouri) on "The Inviolability of Telegrams," a new legal question created by the advance in communications technology; George A. Mercer (Georgia) on "The Relationship of Law and the National Spirit;" and an essay by Calvin G. Child (Connecticut) on "Shifting Uses, from the Standpoint of the Nineteenth Century," which dealt with the flaws and needed remedies of the jury system, its argument supported with historical references reaching from Blackstone back to 27 Henry VIII, Chap. 10.

Such papers and addresses dealing with technical aspects of public and private law, presented by leading figures in the profession, were a continuing feature of the annual meetings throughout the Saratoga period. But the most striking event of the two-day meeting in 1879 and indeed of the Association's brief existence up to that point, came as the result of the selection of Edward J. Phelps, a signer of the original circular letter and a Vermonter of distinction, known for his seamed face, spread of whiskers and legal scholarship, to deliver the first annual address. The banquet was held at the Grand Union Hotel, the perfect setting for old-fashioned dinners and postprandial addresses. On such occasions the speaker put his erudition on display, usually in connection with constitutional topics. Phelps was a man of broad culture, known for his felicity as a public speaker. He chose as his subject Chief Justice Marshall and the constitutional law. The address was something of a tour de force because it was delivered without notes or written text. However, the effort had been prepared with care. According to one who was present, Jacob Weart of New Jersey, the oration was wonderfully delivered, without hesitation, closely reasoned, filled with "luminous judgments" and "unanswerable logic," and so eloquent that Phelps "had the strong minds of the Association at his feet in tears, and I am not ashamed to confess that I was one of the number." The speech was, in short, a sensation. A Democrat in a strong Republican state, Phelps naturally enjoyed little prospect of political advancement at home. But the Democratic members of the ABA who heard the tribute to John Marshall whispered among themselves that the first Democratic vacancy on the Supreme Court of the United States would be his.

Phelps did in fact receive serious consideration for the office of Chief Justice when it became vacant through the death of Morrison R. Waite, but political considerations intervened. President Cleveland had previously recognized Phelps, however, by sending him to the Court of St. James's where he served with conspicuous success. In ABA history Phelps is credited with having elevated the annual address to a "role of great distinction."

Benjamin H. Bristow, the former Secretary of the Treasury, was elected president for 1879–80 and on the evening of August 21, 1879, eighty-six members attended a banquet presided over by John H. B. Latrobe, the versatile Marylander who deserves much more attention than can be accorded him in this brief account. Members responded to a long list of toasts, a total of twelve. The following are representative: "The Legal Profession;" "The Bench;" "The Retiring President;" "The New Administration;" "The American Bar Association;" "The Common Law;" and a curious, jesting topic was elaborated by Anthony Q. Keasbey, United States Attorney for the district of New Jersey. Perhaps Keasbey was the ABA's official funmaker. At any rate, the toast was entitled "The Knowledge of the Titmouse as to the Gestation of the Elephant." There must have been some appropriate connection with the occasion, for Keasbey was a man of taste and charm with a delicate literary touch. But the substance of what he said is unfortunately lost to us.

Memories of the Grand Union Hotel are inextricably linked with the prandial traditions of the ABA. The Grand Union, it was claimed, was the largest or at

Collection of George S. Bolster

The superstar of the great hotels of Saratoga Springs was the Grand Union. Last to fall before the wrecker's ball, the "Union" epitomized the Second Empire architecture and elegance of life at America's most fashionable watering place. The first annual banquets of the ABA were held at the Grand Union. On its spacious piazzas the leaders of the Association met to plan and guide its activities.

least the second-largest hotel in the world. The site occupied seven acres in the center of town, bounded by Broadway, Congress, Federal, and Washington streets. Frequently rebuilt, remodeled, and refurbished, the Grand Union was constructed of yellow brick and iron and located on the ground where the first hotel at the Springs had stood, the building put up in 1802 and known as Putnam's Tavern or later Union Hall. In its days of splendor the Grand Union, or the "Union," as it was called informally, rose three stories high on the Broadway side, overlooking Congress Park and the Congress Spring. The total height was five stories with a central tower surrounded by galleries rising above the rotunda. The verandas added up to a solid mile in length, equipped with a thousand stout wicker rocking chairs. This was luxe and elegance as understood in the Age of Victoria. It was Saratoga Springs's version of American front porch life, but distinctive because of who sat in the chairs and the fact that morning concerts were given al fresco with waiter service on the piazzas to provide refreshing drinks and a majordomo to pick up lost handkerchiefs, umbrellas, and diamonds.

"No noisy railroad, noissome stables and boardinghouse kitchens flank its sides," declared a brochure issued by the Grand Union management—a low blow at the United States Hotel whose porches were, nevertheless, graced by the presence of capitalists whose net worth reached seven ciphers.

Huge archways, centered on the Broadway frontage, framed the main entrance to the Union office. Office and rotunda were paved with red and white marble squares, enough marble to cover an acre. The grand parlor, six patented steam elevators, four black walnut staircases and the private dining rooms were on the left as one entered. The great public dining room, largest in the world, is was said, seating 1200, opened across the corridor to the right, its atmosphere

DINNER.

TUESDAY, AUGUST 19, 1879.

SOUP.

Mutton Broth with Barley. Consommé Sago

FISH.

Boiled Kennebec Salmon with Escalope, à la Poulette.
Baked Blackfish, à l'Espagnole.

BOILED.

Leg of Mutton, Caper sauce. Corned Beef and cabbage
Fresh Ribs of Beef, à la Bourgeoise. Chicken with Smoked Beef Tongue

RELEVEÉS.

Bœuf à la Mode à l'Allemande.
Calf's Feet breaded, sauce Tartare

ENTREÉS.

Filet of Veal breaded, Frite au Nouille.
Calf's Brains en Caisses au Gratin, à l'Italienne.
Haricot of Beef, à l'Alsacienne.
Fricassée of Turkey Wings, à la Toulouse
Escalope of Rice, Vanilla Créme

ROAST.

Ribs of Beef. Spring Lamb, Mint sauce.
Spring Chicken stuffed. Ham glacé, Champagne sauce
Shoulder of Veal stuffed, Tomato sauce.

Guests having friends at meals will please report to Office or Head Waiter.

MAYONNAISE.

Chicken. Lobster. Cucumbers. Tomatoes. Lettuce

COLD DISHES

Ham. Smoked Beef Tongue. Pressed Corned Beef
Spring Chicken. Spring Lamb. Plain Lobster.
Boned Turkey au Truffes Perigord.
Ribs of Beef.

VEGETABLES.

Boiled Bermuda Potatoes. Squash. Bermuda Onions.
Mashed Potatoes. New Beets. Succotash.
Stewed Tomatoes. Boiled Rice.
Green Peas. Cabbage. New Sweet Corn

PASTRY.

Peach Pie. Green Gage Tarts. Blackberry Pie
Indian Pudding, Hard and Rum sauce.
Lady Cakes. Baked Cup Custard, Orange flavor. Snow Flakes
Assorted Cakes. Boston Cream Puffs. Lemon Candy

FRUITS.

Blackberries. Peaches. Watermelon

DESSERT.

Paper-shelled Almonds. English Walnuts. Filberts
Pecan Nuts. Brazil Nuts. Layer Raisins.

VANILLA ICE CREAM. STRAWBERRY WATER ICE.

COFFEE. *TEA.*

Parties desiring permanent seats will please notify Head Waiter.

FULL DRESS HOP THIS EVENING IN BALL ROOM.

A specimen dinner menu from the Grand Union's dining room. And that's how they ate at the Springs in the second year of the ABA's existence! What a convenience: one could get indigestion on one side of Broadway and relief on the other.

Saratoga Springs Historical Society

of invitation enhanced by snowy linen, burnished silver, napkins neatly folded and inserted in the goblets. Fifty items claimed attention on the bill of fare, and 250 waiters stood at attention under the command of a dusky headwaiter of imposing dignity and authority.

From 1872 to his death in 1876, A. T. Stewart, the New York merchant prince, owned the Grand Union, investing a sum in the range of $500,000 to $2,000,000 in improvements, such as all-new walnut furniture, still more verandas, a new landscaping of the interior garden, new frescoes in the public rooms, and the construction of a new white-and-gold ballroom. Three large crystal electric chandeliers were suspended from the ceiling and an enormous allegorical oil painting was installed on the west wall of the ballroom. Generally known as the "Grand Centennial Painting," because it was one of the largest pictures in the world and was mounted in the Centennial year of 1876, the actual title of the work was "The Genius of America." Commissioned in 1870, the painting was the work of a greatly admired French artist, Adolphe Yvon (1817–1893), who painted historical subjects, especially victorious French battle scenes, in an imposing style greatly appreciated by Napoleon III because Yvon's oeuvre served the interest of *la politique impérialiste.*

The picture that arrived at Saratoga depicted America as a beauty of opulent charms dispensing learning, culture, healing and money from a horn of plenty. The painting was admired particularly because of its statistics. It cost $110,000, showed a spread of canvas of 18 x 29½ feet, and with its ornate frame weighed 2500 or some said 3500 pounds. The frame was a marvel of workmanship, *Frank Leslie's Weekly Illustrated Newspaper* said, and the picture was "great," too. It was understood that the painting had been intended for Stewart's private gallery in his Fifth Avenue mansion but was found to be too large for the space. So it went to the Grand Union to adorn the scene of hops, formal balls, concerts, magic shows, and lectures on Christian Science. Happily, Yvon's huge painting still exists. It now hangs in Chancellor's Hall, the auditorium of the New York State Education Department at Albany, and may be seen by appointment with the building superintendent. Unhappily, the Grand Union Hotel no longer exists. It fell before the wrecker's ball in 1952. Its site is now occupied by a shopping center including as its centerpiece a supermarket called—the Grand Union.

It was on the spacious porch of the Union that the early leaders of the American Bar Association relaxed over a chalice of Old Monongahela to discuss the state of the nation, significant new court decisions, such as the Granger Cases, Munn v. Illinois 94 U.S. 113 (1877), or Judge Thomas M. Cooley's influential *Treatise on the Constitutional Limitations Which Rest Upon the Legislative Power of the States of the American Union,* which interpreted the due process clause of the Fourteenth Amendment, Professor Bernard Schwartz has estimated, as "a virtual Magna Carta for business." And perhaps the group of wise and prudent men noticed from time to time the flirt of a skirt as they gazed down the long vista of the piazza. This is a matter of conjecture, a not unpleasant possibility. At least we know that there is no doctrine of the prudent woman, a sugject upon which the law is silent. What we can be sure of, because it is a matter of record, is that this coterie of well-known lawyers, almost a club of intimates, met to decide on a slate of officers for the next year and whom to have for orator to deliver the principal address. And it quickly developed that whomever was chosen for that honor usually was tapped for president in the following year.

A brilliant, willful, truculent man well endowed with enemies, who, however, in good conscience could not be kept out of the presidential succession since he was a towering figure in American jurisprudence in the 1870's was the polished and elegant David Dudley Field. Huge in stature and powerful in intellect, tireless propagandist for codification, an ambitious man, too, Field promoted himself so directly for president of the ABA that on one occasion Broadhead, then on the nominating Council, stopped Field in the hotel and said: "Mr. Field, I came down here in favor of you for president of the American Bar Association. I thought we had to recognize you. But there is one rule that we agreed upon long ago on the porch in Saratoga, and that is that a man who seeks to be president of the American Bar Association cannot be president." Despite his disabilities of temperament, Field's solid achievements eventually outweighed them and he became the eleventh president of the ABA in 1888–89.

Not long after the ABA was successfully launched upon its long career, a restlessness became evident among some of the members regarding the location of the annual meeting. A number of influential lawyers came to feel that Saratoga Springs had pleasured them enough. An attempt was made to go to the Greenbrier Hotel at White Sulphur Springs, West Virginia, but the hotel management said that they could not accomodate so large a group as the ABA in the high season. Charles Carroll Bonney (named after Charles Carroll of Carrollton, the last surviving signer of the Declaration of Independence), member of the Illinois bar and a successful general practitioner, spoke eloquently in favor of Chicago and the facilities of the famous Palmer House. Bonney in his enthusiasm went so far out on a limb as to assert that the summer climate of Chicago was equal to that of Saratoga Springs. And he applied to Chicago Daniel Webster's famous tribute to Massachusetts in saying that he would enter on no encomium upon Chicago; she needs none. There she is.

Bonney's argument was received with a good deal of skepticism, not only as to Chicago's charms in August, but also as to the policy issue involved and the direction which the ABA should take in its development. The Association had been conceived as a voluntary coming together of individuals of known attainments. It was exlcusive rather than representative, somewhat academic in tone, with Rawle, the longtime treasurer, making a career of shaping the banquet program and editing the orations for the printer, while the elder statesmen of the Association tightly controlled the rotation of the offices. Many members liked the combination of business and diversion that Saratoga Springs offered. Hinckley, for example, thought that if about one hundred members attended the meetings they could be conveniently seated at dinner. Larger numbers would create problems and the meetings would become harder to orchestrate. "One hundred is a good round number," Hinckley insisted, "and ordinarily sufficient for social purposes."

So for eleven consecutive years the Springs was the exclusive meeting place of the ABA. Then for the next fourteen years the meetings ordinarily alternated each year between Saratoga and some important city of the United States—including Chicago. At the turn of the century it was clear that moving the annual meetings to various urban locations would best promote the serious objectives of the ABA. Nineteen hundred and two marks the end of the Saratoga Era and therefore of this chronicle about "a very convenient excuse to come to Saratoga." And by the time the twentieth century had arrived, the fear of too many members, including younger men, joining the American Bar Association, had passed away. Only once after that—in 1917—did the ABA return to the place of its birth, gathering at the Grand Union for a last time at a dinner honoring Elihu Root.

Now rounding off a hundred years of growth, of useful work and fruitful influence generated first at Saratoga Springs, the American Bar Association enters its second century with the strength and the will to promote, as old Cotton Mather long ago urged lawyers to do, the felicity of our country.

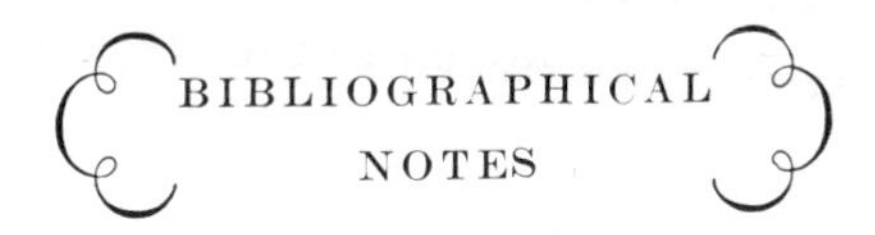

BIBLIOGRAPHICAL NOTES

Materials used in the preparation of this volume appear below. Facts of publication are given in full in the first citation; when repeated, they appear in shortened form.

Abbreviations:

ABA Jour.	American Bar Association Journal
ABA Rep.	American Bar Association Reports
Colo. B.A. Rep.	Colorado Bar Association Reports
Conn. B. Jour.	Connecticut Bar Journal
DAB	Dictionary of American Biography
N.J.L.Jour.	New Jersey Law Journal

Grateful acknowledgment is made of valuable assistance rendered by the Chicago headquarters staff of the ABA; by Mrs. Michael E. Sweeney, City Historian, Saratoga Springs, New York; and by the following libraries: The New-York Historical Society library, the New York Public Library, the New York State Library, and Vassar College Library.

Three participants and observers of the beginnings of the ABA have left accounts of the events of a century ago: Simeon E. Baldwin, "The Founding of the American Bar Association," 3 *ABA Jour.* (October, 1917), pp.658–695; Francis Rawle, "How the Association Was Organized," 14 *ABA Jour.* (1928), pp.375–377; and Jacob Weart, "American Bar Association: Its History for the First Sixteen Years of its Existence and its Impress upon the Thought of the Nation," 27 *N.J.L. Jour.* (1904), pp.292–299. Rawle mentions the beautiful weather and I have checked up on him through the report in the *Albany Journal*, August 21, and 22, 1878.

Contemporary documents: "Call for a Meeting to Form an American Bar Association. Proceedings of the Conference Called for the Purpose of Organizing a National Bar Association, and of the First Annual Meeting of the American Bar Association," *ABA Rep.* Vols. 1–5 (Philadelphia: 1878), pp.5–35. This work, as indicated, is a collection of the official records for the first five years of the ABA's existence.

Modern writers on the founding of the Association include Max Radin, "The Achievements of the American Bar Association: A Sixty Year Record," 25 *ABA Jour.* (November, 1939), pp.904–907; James Grafton Rogers, "Fifty Years of the American Bar Association," 14 *ABA Jour.* (1928), pp.521–525; Edson R. Sunderland, *History of the American Bar Association and its Work* (n.p., 1953), based chiefly on *ABA Rep.;* and Bernard Schwartz, *The American Heritage History of the Law in America* (American Heritage Publishing Co., 1974). Two engaging accounts of the venerable symbol of parliamentary authority, the mallet/gavel, are: "Colloquy Between James Grafton Rogers and John W. Davis," 52 *ABA Rep.* (1927), pp.42–43; and Rogers Platt, "The Story of the Carpenter's Mallet," 30 *Colo. B.A. Rep.* (1927), pp.116–120.

Biographical information and characterizations of the early leaders of the Association will be found in James Grafton Rogers, *American Bar Leaders: Biographies of the Presidents of the American Bar Association* (Chicago: The American Bar Association, 1932). Most are also subjects of essays in the *Dictionary of American Biography* with bibliographies attached to each sketch. For Baldwin see *Records & Addresses in Memory of Simeon E. Baldwin: 1840–1927* (New Haven, 1928), James Grafton Rogers, "History of the American Bar Association," 39 *ABA Jour.* (August, 1953), p.660; and Victor M. Gordon et al, "A History of the First One Hundred Years of the Connecticut Bar Association: 1875–1975," 49 *Conn. B. Jour.*, (June, 1975). A full-length biography is Frederick H. Jackson, *Simeon Eben Baldwin: Lawyer, Social Scientist, Statesman* (New York: King's Crown Press, Columbia University, 1955).

Popular attitudes of resistance to the common law and lawyers are discussed and illustrated from documentary sources in Michael Kammen, *Colonial New York: A History* (New York: Scribner, 1975). I paraphrase and quote from a rare and incendiary pamphlet, Frederic Robinson, *A Letter to the Hon. Rufus Choate, Containing a Brief Exposure of Law Craft, and Some of the Encroachments of the Bar Upon the Rights and Liberties of the People* (n.p., 1832), p.11, and cite the 1851 Indiana State Constitution from Charles Kettleborough, *Constitution Making in Indiana: A Source Book of Constitutional Documents with Historical Introduction and Critical Notes.* Indiana Historical Collections. (Indianapolis: Indiana Historical Commission, 1916)1:346.

My treatment of early law clubs and associations in England and colonial America, and the developing state associations of the nineteenth century, rest upon Gordon, "*History of the First One Hundred Years of the Connecticut Bar Association,*" p. 203; Roscoe Pound, *The Lawyer from Antiquity to Modern Times with Particular Reference to the Development of Bar Associations in the United States: A Study Prepared for and Published by the Survey of the Legal Profession Under the Auspices of the American Bar Association* (St. Paul, Minnesota: West Publishing Co., 1953), pp.8,12–14,189, *passim;* William Makepeace Thackeray, *The History of Pendennis* (New York: Harper & Brothers, 1903), p.283.

The number of lawyers in the United States *circa* 1878 will be found in *U.S. Bureau of the Census, 1880*. Pt. 2. Table xxxi, p.733.

The story of Saratoga Springs early and late, its geology, its visitors distinguished and otherwise, the vivacity of the social life, all may be studied in a copious literature of strangers' guides, promotional brochures, personal reminiscences, humorous and poetical works, social histories and newspapers. An incomplete list of fugitive and enduring works which I consulted includes: Cleveland Amory, *The Last Resorts* (New York: Harper & Brothers, 1952); E. Bénézit, *Dictionnaire critique et documentaire des Peintres, Sculpteurs, Dessinateurs et Graveurs* . . . 8(Paris: Librarie Gründ, 1960), p.829; J.S. Buckingham, *America, Historical, Statistic, and Descriptive.* 3 vols. (London: 1841)2:429–436, 444–445; J. Sullivan, Alexander C. Flick and M.W. Hamilton, ed., *The Papers of Sir William Johnson.* 13 vols. (Albany: The University of the State of New York, 1933) 8:258; James Thomas Flexner, *George Washington in the American Revolution, 1775–1783* (Boston: Little, Brown & Co., 1968); Douglas Southall Freeman, *George Washington: A Biography.* 7 vols. (New York: Scribner, 1948–1957)5:450; *Grand Union Hotel: Season 1890* (Saratoga Springs, N.Y., 1890); Robert Gray Gunderson, *The Log-Cabin Campaign* (University of Kentucky Press); (Marietta Holley), *Samantha at Saratoga, or "Flirtin' with Fashion," by Josiah Allen's Wife* (Philadelphia: Hubbard Brothers, 1887); John C. Kirkpatrick, ed., *The Writings of George Washington from the Original Sources, 1745–1799.* 39 vols. (Washington, D.C.: U.S. Govt. Print. Off., 1931–1944) 27:65,67,99–100, 501; (Henry Lee), *Lee's Guide to Saratoga, the Queen of Spas* (New York, 1885); (Melville De Lancey Landon), *Saratoga in 1901. By Eli Perkins* (pseud.). *Fun. Love. Society & Satire* (New York: 1872); George Martin, *Causes and Conflicts: The Centennial History of the Association of the Bar of the City of New York 1870–1970* (Boston: Houghton Mifflin Co., 1970); *New York: A Guide to the Empire State.* American Guide Series. (New York: Oxford University Press, 1940); Frank Presbrey, *A Summer Paradise* (n.p., *circa* 1900); *Report of the Committee on Legal Education and Admissions to the Bar, of the American Bar Association, read at the Annual Meeting of the Association, Saratoga Springs, N.Y., August 21, 1879* (Philadelphia, 1879); J. Smith, *Reminiscences of Saratoga, or*

Twelve Seasons at the "States" (New York: 1897); *Saratoga Illustrated: The Visitor's Guide to Saratoga Springs . . .* (New York, 1878), with map; *Saratoga Springs: "The Gift of the Great Spirit," "The D&H"* (n.p., n.d.); John Godfrey Saxe, *The Poetical Works of John Godfrey Saxe* (1882), p.49; *The State Reservation at Saratoga Springs: An Historical and Descriptive Statement of the Mineral Springs and Baths Owned and Operated by the State of New York* (Albany: State of New York Conservation Commission, 1917); William Leete Stone, *Reminiscences of Saratoga and Ballston* (New York, 1875); *A Souvenir of Saratoga Springs, New York* (n.p., n.d.); (Charles Newhall Taintor), *Taintor's New York Central and Hudson Railway* (New York, 1874); Charles E. Trevathan, *Saratoga's Sports and Splendors* Reprint from *Everybody's Magazine*, (August, 1904); Bayard Tuckerman, ed., *The Diary of Philip Hone 1828–1851.* 2 vols. (New York: Dodd, Mead & Co., 1889); George Waller, *Saratoga: Saga of an Impious Era* (New York: Bonanza Books, 1966); Dixon Wecter, *The Saga of American Society: A Record of Social Aspiration 1607–1937* (New York: Scribner, 1937).

Various issues of the following newspapers were useful: *Albany Times-Union; Frank Leslie's Illustrated Newspaper; New York Herald; New York Daily Tribune; New York Times; Newark Daily Advertiser; Saratoga Springs Saratogian; Wilkes' Spirit of the Times.*

The end of the "Saratoga Era" may be traced in *Report of the Sixth Annual Meeting of the American Bar Association, held at Saratoga Springs, New York, Aug. 22, 23, and 24, 1883* (Philadelphia, 1883); Rogers, *American Bar Leaders*, p.123; 74 *ABA Rep.* (1949), p.563; 5 *ABA Rep.* (1882), pp.7,15,64; 6 *ABA Rep.* (1883), pp.6,47,49, all quoted in Sunderland, *History*, pp.34–41; and in 3 *ABA Jour.* (1917), p.631.